On London & North Western Lines

Derek Huntriss

First published 1995

ISBN 07110 23824

© Derek Huntriss 1995

Designed by Derek Huntriss

Published by Ian Allan Publishing

an imprint of Ian Allan Ltd, Terminal House, Station Approach, Shepperton, Surrey TW17 8AS; and printed by Ian Allan Printing Ltd., Coombelands House, Coombelands Lane, Addlestone, Weybridge, Surrey KT15 1HY.

Front Cover:
'Britannia' Pacific No 70023 *Venus* heads an express for Shrewsbury through Whitchurch in August 1963.
D. Penney

Rear Cover:
LNWR Class G2A 0-8-0 No 49361 has been cleaned up for the occasion of an SLS railtour on 22 June 1963 and is depicted south of Lichfield near Shenstone.
R. Hobbs

This Page:
'Britannia' Pacific No 70013 *Oliver Cromwell* has been groomed by the MNA enthusiast group for what became the last steam hauled passenger working over Shap - a football supporters' special from Carlisle to Blackpool on 26 December 1967, which is seen approaching Shap village.
Paul Riley

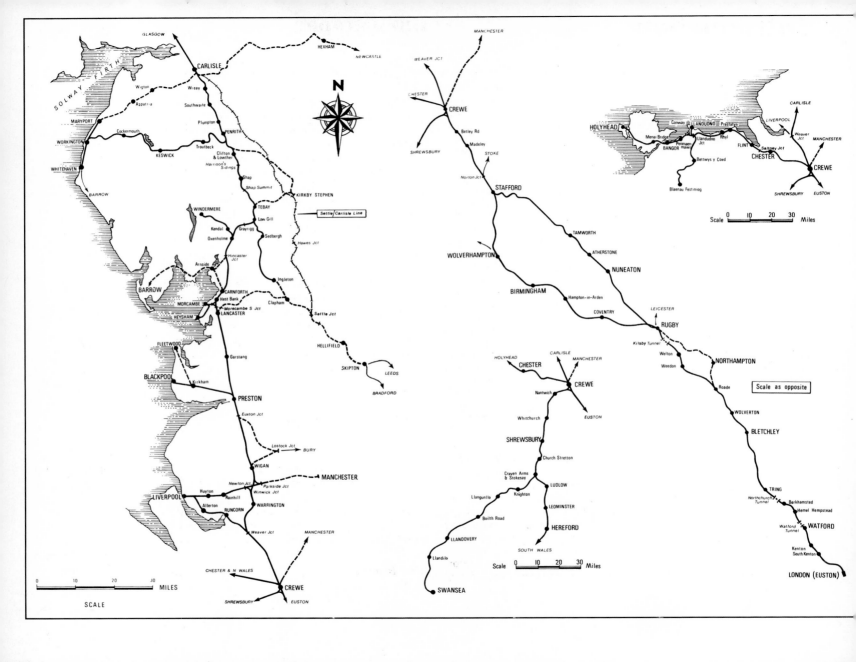

Introduction

In its heyday, The London & North Western Railway, the 'Premier Line' of Great Britain, was the largest undertaking in the country. The company had been created by the amalgamation on 1 January 1846 of the London & Birmingham (L&B), the Grand Junction Railway (GJR) and the Manchester & Birmingham (M&B). Over the next fifty years the LNWR went from strength to strength.

Recorded in an interview for the *Railway Magazine* in September 1897, the company's General Manager, Mr Frederick Harrison, stated that the LNWR was commonly believed to be the biggest joint-stock corporation in the world. In the same interview he confirmed that the company's authorised capital stood at £120,000,000 and gross revenue for the previous year had been twelve million and a half. In the same year the company had carried over one hundred million passengers and over forty million tons of goods, the company employing no fewer than seventy thousand people.

Its main lines boasted splendid engineering works and a superb permanent way. A West Coast express of 80 years ago was a fine sight with its capacious twelve-wheelers, immaculate in their plum and off-white, headed by a 'Claughton' or a 'George the Fifth' in highly polished black.

On studying a railway map from that period, it was easy to perceive that the London & North Western, which extended nearly all over the country from London in the south to Carlisle in the north, to Holyhead in the west, and to Leeds in the northeast, had its central pivot at Crewe. In June 1904, an LNWR official, Mr S.M. Phillp, reflected on Crewe's further expansion in the *Railway Magazine* - "It had long been established as one of Britain's great railway towns." When the borough had celebrated its Jubilee in 1887, a lavishly produced history published by the *Crewe Guardian* noted its phenomenal growth.

In 1923, the LNWR was absorbed into the London, Midland & Scottish Railway which existed until 1947, the latter also claiming to be the largest company in Britain, if not the world.

Whilst many of the locomotive types shown in this title were constructed by the LMS, and later BR, some LNWR types that survived into the 1950s and 1960s period are also depicted. Two working preserved examples of LNWR motive power are also illustrated. The title is roughly divided into two parts. The first taking the reader on a journey from Euston to Carlisle, and the second exploring other former LNWR lines which have not hitherto seen extensive coverage in colour.

Bibliography

Rex Christiansen: *Rail Centres – Crewe;* Ian Allan
C.J. Gammell: *LMS Branch Lines;* GRQ Publications
P.B. Hands: *What Happened to Steam – Vols 1 to 30;* P.B. Hands.
Chris Hawkins, John Hooper & George Reeve: *British Railways Engine Sheds – London Midland Matters;* Irwell Press.
Peter Hay: *Pre-Grouping Trains on British Railways – The LMS Companies;* Oxford Publishing Company.
Alex Henley: *Names & Nameplates of British Steam Locomotives – 1. LMS & Constituents;* Heyday Publishing Company
D. Huntriss: *The Colour of Steam – Vol 6: The LMS Pacifics;* Atlantic Transport Publishing Co.
Peter Lee; *The Trent Valley Railway (Rugby-Stafford 1847-1966);* Trent Valley Publications
Keith Robey & Raymond J. Green; *Steam around Nuneaton;* Midland Counties Publications
Paul Smith: *The Handbook of Steam Motive Power Depots – Vols 1 to 4,* Platform 5 Publishing Co.
Edward Talbot: *Railways in and around Stafford;* Foxline Publishing
Edward Talbot: *The LNWR Recalled;* OPC
Magazines: *Backtrack; Modern Railways; Railway Magazine; Railway World: Steam Railway; Steam World; The World of Trains; Trains Illustrated*

Acknowledgements

Thanks are offered to all the dedicated photographers whose work appears in these pages. Without their efforts in pioneering the use of slow colour film many years ago and storing their irreplaceable images in good condition over the intervening period, this title could not have been contemplated. I must also give sincere thanks to Bryan Wilson of the LNWR Society for sharing his in-depth knowledge of the subject.

Derek Huntriss

Camborne
Cornwall
March 1995

Allocated to Camden (1B) MPD for much of her working life, Stanier Pacific No 46239 *City of Chester* awaits departure from Euston with the 4.45pm to Liverpool Lime Street on 27 July 1962. At this time work on the first phase of the Euston rebuilding had already begun in April 1962. By April 1966 work was virtually complete, a minimum of 11 platforms being maintained in use throughout the reconstruction project. Reconstruction had been under consideration for more than 50 years, the final British Railways £15 million design bearing a striking resemblance to an LMSR proposal of 1935. The rebuilt station was formally opened by Her Majesty the Queen on 14 October 1968.

G. Rixon

Carrying the later BR style livery with the lining at the panel edges, Stanier Pacific No 46238 *City of Carlisle* is being turned on Camden's 70ft vacuum-operated turntable before being switched to the appropriate shed road. A 4 August 1962 picture. The sequence of loco- motive disposal operations at Camden was 1.Watering 2. Coaling 3. Dropping fire. 4. Turning. 5. Inspection prior to disposal in shed. These operations at Camden were thought to be the model for an LMS Traffic Committee proposal of 24 May 1933 for the wholesale modernisation of its engine sheds. Camden MPD closed to steam operations on 9 September 1963, total closure coming on 3 January 1966. Today the buildings are demolished and the site occupied by sidings.

G. Rixon

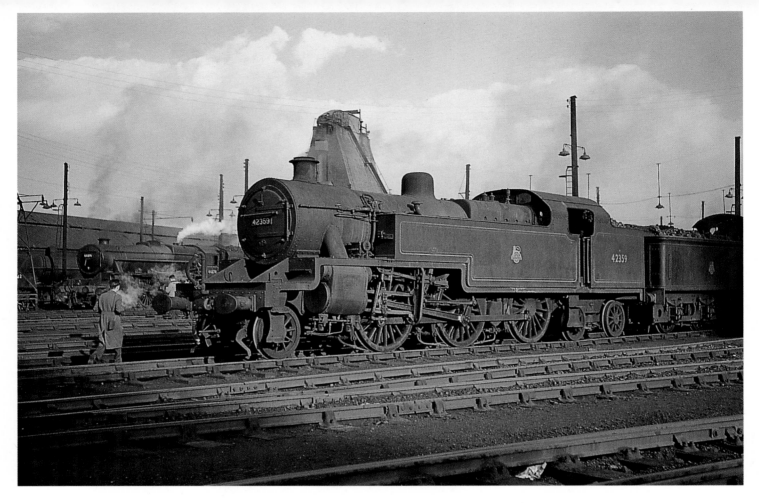

Above:

During her 22 months' allocation to Willesden (1A) MPD Fowler 2-6-4T No 42359 is depicted at that depot on 15 March 1959. By August of that year No 42359 had been despatched to Northwich (8E) MPD. Willesden MPD was more notable for what it had lost rather than for any improvements. An entire new shed in northlight style had once stood in front of the old hipped roof building that survived into the 1960s. The former building was possibly the only large LNWR building to be demolished before the end of steam operations. It was also famous for its ill-fated 'pneumatic smokebox ash extractor' – a device tried with a similar lack of success at the neighbouring GWR depot at Old Oak Common. *W.Potter*

Right:

The crew of 'Britannia' Pacific No 70021 *Morning Star,* chat at the water column as they prepare her for her next duty at Willesden MPD on 9 October 1963. At this time Willesden was home to no fewer than 14 'Britannias', six of these having had their duties at March (31B) MPD displaced by Darnall (41A) MPD´s English Electric Type 3 diesels. *G. Rixon*

Following the closure of Camden (1B) MPD in September 1963 and before the 25kV wires were fully energised from Euston in 1964, Willesden MPD (formerly used mainly for freight duties) became the only London area steam depot for the old LNWR main line. The remaining LMS passenger types which had been allocated to Camden, now found themselves side by side with the more humble freight locomotives. Here Stanier Pacific No 46240 *City of Coventry* stands out from the crowd on 8 March 1964. One of the last 'Coronation' Class Pacifics to be withdrawn from traffic, *City of Coventry* ran the highest mileage of all the Stanier Pacifics – 1,685,000. After various preservation attempts, No 46240 met her end at Cashmore's yard at Great Bridge, Tipton, Staffs. The only parts that remain are its nameplates and crest. One set can be found adorning the rebuilt Coventry station, the other in private ownership. As for Willesden MPD, it was closed on 27 September 1965 and was demolished in December 1966.

W. Potter

By the late 19th century the popularity of the family holiday was growing and it was not long before the resorts along the south coast were becoming popular with visitors from the Midlands and the North. After World War 2 the 'Sunny South Special' virtually ceased to exist. However, from 1949 a Saturdays-only train ran from Birmingham and Coventry to Brighton and Hastings and continued in this form until 1963. Here, Stanier Class 5 No 44873 heads the SO 11.5am from Walsall to Hastings over Castlethorpe troughs on 30 August 1958, the last operational Saturday of the summer timetable.   *T. B. Owen*

Left: This superb action shot depicts 'Patriot' No 45518 *Bradshaw* as its heads the up 'Mancunian' over Castlethorpe troughs on 30 August 1958. Built at Crewe in February 1933, this engine was nominally a rebuild of 'Claughton.' No 6006 whose number it carried until 1934. However, this was an accountancy manoeuvre; the engines being new ones built for a corresponding number of small-boilered

'Claughton' withdrawals. Like most classes designed for express passenger work, the 'Patriots' came to be used on virtually all types of traffic, their allocations on the LMS/LMR system were as far apart as Carlisle and Bristol Barrow Road. The 'Patriots', always associated with the West Coast main line, were for much of the 1930s the prime motive power on the Midland Division.
T. B. Owen

Above: Bushbury (3B) MPD's Stanier Class 5 No 45439 takes water from Bushey troughs as it heads a rake of former LMS stock carrying Wolverhampton Wanderers' supporters to the F.A. Cup Final at Wembley on 7 May 1960. They returned home jubilant as Wolves had beaten Blackburn Rovers 3-0. Bushey troughs was one of 11 sets on the West Coast main line between Euston and Glasgow.
T. B. Owen

13

Above: The driver of Johnson Midland 0-6-0 No 58288 poses for the camera at Rugby in April 1954. The former Midland Railway's route from Leicester to Rugby was opened on 30 June 1840 as part of the Midland Counties Railway. At that time it was the principal route to the North East prior to the construction of the East Coast main line. After the Midland had extended southwards from Leicester, the line became a secondary cross-country route and was closed by BR to passenger and freight on 1 January 1962. Of the stations extant, Ullesthorpe is the most interesting as it is still complete and has been lovingly restored by its owners in LMS maroon and white. *J. M. Jarvis*

Right: Ex-LMS 'Patriot' No 45503 *The Royal Leicestershire Regiment* heads towards the former Great Central Railway's 'Birdcage' bridge as it leaves Rugby station with an up working in 1954. The word *Royal* was added to the nameplate of No 45503 in November 1948, the engine receiving new double line plates incorporating the alteration. *J. M. Jarvis*

Left: Rebuilt 'Patriot' No 45535 *Sir Herbert Walker K.C.B.* arrives at Rugby with an up express in 1953. Unlike the LMS 'Royal Scot' class 4-6-0s whose names followed a formal sequence of British Regiments and military associations, Sir Henry Fowler's Class 5XP 4-6-0 'Patriots' or 'Baby Scots' (as they later became known) received a more random choice of names which ranged from senior officers and General Managers of the London & North Western Railway to Welsh coastal resorts served by the LMS, not forgetting to commemorate the exploits of Coventry's legendary Lady Godiva. Sir Herbert Walker whose name was borne by No 45535, was a General Manager of the LNWR who later went on to become General Manager of the London & South Western, later Southern Railway. *J. M. Jarvis*

Above: Newly-constructed BR Standard Class 4 2-6-0 No 76016 *en route* from Horwich Works to its first allocation at Eastleigh (71A) MPD in May 1953, awaits access to the coaling plant at Rugby MPD. This class of locos, totalling 115, designed at Doncaster, were built with light axle loadings giving them wide route availability. *J. M. Jarvis*

Two contrasting studies of the very last express passenger locomotive built for British Railways. Here, No 71000 *Duke of Gloucester* is seen among a convoy of locomotives being towed dead to Willesden for exhibition as part of the 16th International Railway Congress held in London in May 1954. The IRC Honorary President was HRH the Duke of Gloucester who officially named the locomotive after himself. In July 1954 the 'Duke' took up heavy passenger duties on the West Coast main line and was stationed at Crewe North. These duties were included in a link which comprised several 'Duchesses' working the 'Midday Scot' which was a speciality for several years.

J. M. Jarvis

Some eight years later on 15 June 1962, No 71000 is only six months away from the end of her working life on BR. Here, she is seen leaving Rugby with the 11.45am Euston-Crewe, eight coaches for Birmingham having been detached in the station. After 12 years' intense effort by volunteers on the Great Central Railway, No 71000 took to the rails again in fine style in October 1986 and is now one of the stars of the preservation scene. *Peter J. Fitton*

Above: Burton (16F) MPD's Stanier 8F 2-8-0 No 48056 leaves Nuneaton on the former LNWR & Midland Joint Line towards Shackerstone on 23 April 1966. Following cessation of freight traffic on this section from 1971, a society was formed to reopen the line between Shackerstone and Market Bosworth, services commencing on 26 March 1978. *T. B. Owen*

Right: 350hp diesel shunter No 12047 is alongside Ivatt 2-6-0 No 46512 outside Nuneaton (5E) MPD on 15 May 1966. Closing one month later, the depot at Nuneaton had served the surrounding coal-mining industry as well as the the large granite workings just north of the town. Adding to this the proximity of Coventry, with its busy engineering industries and

nearby Hinckley with its own goods yard, it can be seen that there was much potential local and long distance freight working. Much of this activity occurred during hours of darkness when the main lines were virtually free of passenger traffic. This work was principally undertaken by the three hundred or so men based at Nuneaton during these antisocial hours. *N. Fields*

Left: Stanier Pacific No 46239 *City of Chester* rounds the curve west of Milford & Brocton as it heads the down 'Mid-Day Scot' on Sunday 14 September 1958. In the 1920s the fast lines were in the centre and the slow lines on either side. This arrangement was changed when the route was electrified to conform with that north of Stafford where the fast lines are on the Up side and the slow lines on the Down.   *M. Mensing*

Above: A delightful study of Nuneaton (2B) MPD's Stanier Mogul No 42958 as it stands outside the depot at Stafford on 17 February 1963. The first stage of modernisation at Stafford came in the late 1930s when the LMS implemented its programme of shed modernisation to reduce costs and improve efficiency. The new ash pit arrangements were a great advance on those of LNWR days when ashes were dropped anywhere in the yard and cleared away by labourers with barrows. The next stage of modernisation was the rebuilding of No 2 shed, the most noticeable feature being its replacement roof visible in this picture. Quite surprisingly, the building survives today, and with another replacement roof it is in commercial use as The Palmbourne Industrial Park.   *A. N. H. Glover*

En route from the Southern Region to its new home at Llandudno Junction (6G) MPD, Standard Class 2 2-6-2 No 84022 shunts stock at Crewe station on 22 September 1961. This class of 30 engines, introduced in 1953, was designed to replace the ageing classes of pre-grouping 2-4-2 and 0-4-4 tanks on branch line passenger work. To enable these locomotives to work push-pull trains, they were fitted with vacuum-controlled auxiliary regulator valves which were fitted in each steam pipe from the super-heater header to the cylinders. Other features included self-cleaning smoke-boxes, rocking grates and hopper ashpans to make life as easy as possible for the depot staff. Some members of the class had a working life of only seven years. Whilst there was a plan to replace the ageing 'O2s' on the Isle of Wight, this never happened. *W. Potter*

Carrying the yellow restriction stripes on her cabsides, 'Coronation' Class Pacific No 46245 *City of London* departs from Crewe station at the head of an Ian Allan Railtour on 1 September 1964. Less than one month later No 46256 *Sir William A. Stanier, F.R.S.* dropped its fire and the class was extinct. As part of a BR publicity exercise in 1958, No 46245 was the first to receive the BR maroon livery with yellow and black lining. *City of London* was put on display at Euston on 8 January 1958 alongside No 46250 *City of Lichfield* in green livery so that comparisons could be made.

W. Potter

Below: Crewe Works shunter, 3F 0-6-0T 'Jinty' No 47597, is depicted outside Crewe Works on 13 October 1963. Introduced by the LMS in 1924, this ubiquitous class of shunting locomotives was based on a Johnson design of 1899 with detail alterations, 415 being built for the LMS and seven for the S&DJR. *A. N. H. Glover*

Right: Ex-Works Rebuilt 'Royal Scot' No 46170 *British Legion* backs into Crewe station ready to work an up train on 25 September 1961. Surviving until the end of 1962, No 6170 was originally built by the North British Locomotive Company as an experimental three-cylinder compound in 1929. Using a super-pressure

Schmidt boiler, No 6399 *Fury* never entered service. Whilst on trials in February 1930, one of the super-pressure water tubes burst at Carstairs, killing an inspector and injuring the fireman. Laid aside for five years it was later rebuilt as a conventional, but improved, 'Royal Scot' with tapered boiler. *W. Potter*

Barrow (12C) MPD's Class 5 No 44882 heads an up Class 5 freight over Moore troughs, between Weaver Junction and Warrington, in August 1966. From 18 June 1962 the BR train classification code utilising the 10 capital letters from A to K was replaced by a revised numerical system using figures from 0 to 9. The code 5 replaced the Class D code which indicated that the train was an Express Freight, livestock, perishable or ballast train with not fewer than 50 per cent vacuum-braked vehicles piped to the engine. Class 5 No 44882 was delivered new to Carlisle Kingmoor (68A & 12A) MPD and apart from its allocation to Barrow (12E & 12C) MPD from June 1961 until December 1966, it had spent most of its working life operating from that depot.

Paul Riley

Another Stanier Class 5, this time Carnforth (10A) MPD's No 45390, is seen heading an unidentified up passenger working, ahead of the Royal Scot, ¾ mile south of Wigan North Western on Sunday 13 June 1965. No 45390 was fortunate to remain in traffic at Carnforth until the end of BR steam on 4 August 1968. The author well remembers the night of 1 August 1968 spent cleaning this machine before it worked the next day's 6.10am goods to Ulverston. *M. Mensing*

Left: Stanier 2-cylinder Class 4P 2-6-4T No 42567, is seen south of Leyland as it heads the 5.45pm Preston to Wigan stopper in September 1964. No 2567 was one of a batch of 73 built by the North British Locomotive Co. Ltd in 1936/7, under maker's order No. L896, and works Nos 24301-73. Stanier used two, three and four cylinders over the range of his designs, and was sometimes regarded as being inconsistent for doing so. The reasons for these variations are easy to discover.

With only one exception he adhered to the two cylinder plan where sufficient power could be obtained from moderate cylinder diameter. For the larger engines he adopted one or two extra cylinders in accordance with the power required – the only exception being the 3-cylinder 2-6-4Ts where it was desired to use the full weight for adhesion.   *D. Penney*

Above: Condensing 'Jinty' 3F 0-6-0 pilots '0F' 0-4-0ST No 47008 back to Lostock Hall MPD past the former Preston (24K) MPD on 11 March 1964. No 47008 had spent the morning shunting at Greenbank sidings and had to be piloted because it was too short to operate the track circuiting. This manoeuvre was not necessary when this was a 24K duty, a task formerly entrusted to Drummond CR 0-4-0ST 'Pug' No 56027.

Peter Fitton

Crewe North (5A) MPD's work-stained 'Jubilee' No 45726 *Vindictive* heads a down passenger working near Morecambe South Junction in June 1963. Early members of the class were considered to be inferior to the 'Patriots' mainly because their steaming was not reliable and their coal and water consumptions were higher. Because of these problems, the 'Jubilees' were unable to take over the accelerated Euston to Birmingham services in 1935. Two main problems were identified. Firstly the blastpipe and chimney proportions needed redesigning and a low degree of superheat was causing inefficient use of steam. Ultimately a modified boiler with a shortened barrel and sloping throatplate firebox, 24 element superheater was adopted. After their first troubled two years the 'Jubilees' came into their own, the modified boiler being fitted to the last 78 engines built, from No 5665 onwards and retrospectively to a small number of the earlier engines. The first member of the class No 45637 *Windward Islands* was withdrawn in 1952 as a result of the Harrow disaster, the class remaining otherwise intact until 1960, by which time they had been reclassified as 6P, the final members surviving until November 1967.

D. Penney

In the final year of steam operations over Shap to Carlisle, 'Britannia' Pacific No 70051 *Firth of Forth* heads 1M38, the 2pm Glasgow to Liverpool, past Hincaster on 19 August 1967. Apart from the retention of No 70013 *Oliver Cromwell* for excursion duty, December 1967 also marked the end of the 'Britannia' Pacifics. No 70051 was one of a batch of 10 constructed at Crewe in 1954 and was fitted with the BR1D flush-sided tenders which had steam-operated coal pushers, 4,725 gallon water capacity and room for 9 tons of coal. A revised cab/tender arrangement was adopted to improve cab comfort   *Peter J. Fitton*

Left: The impressive scenery of the Lune Gorge is a classic setting for this dramatic picture, dated 28 September 1964. It depicts an unidentified freight as it heads south through the gorge in the shadow of Langdale Fell, which rises to 1,925ft above sea level. The river, flowing swiftly between massive rocks, is sandwiched between the mountains. To the west are the Borrowdale Fells (not to be confused with those in Lakeland) with Jeffrey´s mount rising to over 1,000ft. To the east are the Howgills, an amazingly unknown and little visited range of hills. The railway blended well with the landscape, whereas the greater scale of the motorway has destroyed the dramatic effect.

T. B. Owen

Above: Another dramatic picture, this time portraying a BR Standard Class 4 banker working past Greenholme as it assists a freight to Shap summit in the last month of steam working, December 1967. The uncharacteristic cleanliness of this locomotive can be attributed to the overnight activities of the MNA enthusiast group at Tebay MPD.

Paul Riley

Above: The crew of BR Standard Class 4 No 75030 pose for the camera as it banks a train towards the summit near Shap Wells on 4 November 1967. On an autumn day such as this with the mists still lying in the valley bottoms and the noise of cars travelling along the A6 hidden behind the next hill, it was only the distant crowing of whistles at Tebay that broke the silence. The muffled exhausts of Stanier 5 No 45353 and the Standard 4 banker could be heard until they rounded the corner at Greenholme when their efforts became more pronounced and remained audible until the banker was detached at the summit.   *D. Huntriss*

Right: Some two years earlier in October 1965, banking duties were entrusted to Fairburn 2-6-4Ts. Here, No 42225 nears the summit as it banks a Ford car carrier near the summit. An assortment of Anglias and Anglia estates is on its way to the new car-owning generation of the 1960s.   *R. Hobbs*

Below: Stanier Class 5 No 45148 heads the 2pm Glasgow to Liverpool past the former LNWR Standard Type 5 signalbox at Thrimby Grange on 31 July 1965. In general, the LNWR went in for boxes with massive brick lower storeys, with wood construction above floor level, plain gable end and no ornamental nonsense.

Peter J. Fitton

Right: The mists have just risen over Strickland Woods on 26 December 1967 as 'Britannia' Pacific No 70013 *Oliver Cromwell* heads a Carlisle to Blackpool football excursion on the southern ascent to Shap summit. No 70013 had been returned to Ex-Works condition overnight at Carlisle Kingmoor (12A) MPD by

members of the MNA enthusiast group for this journey which became the last steam-hauled passenger train over Shap. On the return journey, *Oliver Cromwell* stopped at Tebay for banking assistance. None being available, it made a spectacular unassisted ascent of Shap with its 451 ton train.

Paul Riley

A classic action shot depicting Carlisle Kingmoor (12A) MPD's well-groomed 'Britannia' Pacific No 70045 *Lord Rowallan* as it nears Shap station with a Carlisle to Manchester Red Bank parcels in December 1967. Monday 1 January 1968 was the date which announced the opening of a new diesel depot simply known as Carlisle. In turn this meant the complete closure of Carlisle Kingmoor MPD and brought to an end the regular use of steam traction over Shap and the Settle & Carlisle routes. *Lord Rowallan's* final duty was to haul the 1.10pm Carlisle to Skipton goods on 30 December 1967, the last steam hauled freight to leave Carlisle before Kingmoor depot was closed.

Paul Riley

Stanier Class 5 No 45055 pilots 'Jubilee' No 45742 *Connaught* as they prepare to leave Penrith with the 2pm Glasgow to Liverpool on 1 August 1964 while an Ivatt Class 2 shunts in the platform for the CK&PR

The Cockermouth, Keswick and Penrith Railway was for many years an important rail link between the industrial areas of West Cumberland and the North East. Most railways sponsored in Cumberland had

mineral traffic as their mainstay and this was coke westbound and pig iron/iron ore eastbound, North Eastern Railway locomotives and men working through to Cockermouth.   *C. J. Gammell*

Left: Stanier Class 5 No 44879 and BR 'Clan' No 72002 *Clan Campbell* blow off as they prepare to depart from Carlisle Citadel with the 2pm Glasgow to Liverpool on 9 September 1960. Until the advent of diesel motive power, Carlisle was always an important engine-changing point. In pre-Grouping days each company had its own locomotive depot. The LNWR was at Upperby, the NBR at Canal, the GSWR and M&CR at Currock Junction, the NER at London Road, the MR at Durran Hill and the CR at Kingmoor. The scene at Citadel with the varied liveries of these companies' locomotives is today unimaginable. *T. B. Owen*

Above: Three years later at Citadel on 10 August 1963, Upperby (12B) MPD's Ivatt Class 2 No 46455 has attached an extra coach to a southbound express. Also in 1963 BR undertook a wholesale reorganisation of Carlisle's goods yards with the opening of one large yard at Kingmoor. *W. Potter*

Above: Stanier '8F' 2-8-0 No 48077 is working a Sunday permanent way train at Ridgmont, between Bletchley and Bedford in 1965. The line is still in use today and has some interesting relics from pre-LMS days. Ridgmont station has an LNWR open frame on the platform and is a one-man operated station. The stations on the Bedford and Bletchley line were constructed in the 'Half-Timbered Gothic' style at the insistence of the Duke of Bedford whose estates the line traversed. Whilst these buildings still exist some are in a poor state of repair. In December 1905 the LNWR introduced a steam railmotor service and opened seven new halts. Some of these closed in 1926, the quaintly named Husborne Crawley, Wootton Pillinge, Wootton Broadmead, and Kempston & Elstow halts are now but a memory although Bow Brickhill, Aspley Guise and Kempston Hardwick survive today, being served by a Network Southeast DMU. *R. Hobbs*

Right: Three days before the withdrawal of passenger services between Northampton and Peterborough, on 1 May 1964, Stanier 2-6-0 No 42946 leaves Wellingborough (London Road) with the 4.53pm departure for Northampton. This type of locomotive was unusual at Wellingborough other than the occasional appearance on shed after working a freight via Wigston from Nuneaton. *K. Fairey*

Left: Driver 'Neighbour' White and Fireman D. Ashley bring Ivatt 2-6-2T No 41227 into Wellingborough London Road with the 8.10am motor working from Northampton on 29 April 1964. Today, the stations at Wellingborough London Road, Ditchford and Irthlingborough having been demolished, the village at Ditchford was noted at one time as having the smallest population in the country – 4.   *K. Fairey*

Above: On the penultimate day of passenger operations No 41225 is at Wellingborough London Road with the same working. The cross-country line from Northampton to Peterborough was opened as a branch of the London & Birmingham on 2 June 1845 and, being the first railway in the area, was built well before the Midland or Great Northern main lines. Freight services between Northampton and Wellingborough were

withdrawn on 6 June 1966; Irthlingborough to Thrapston on 7 June 1965; Thrapston Bridge to Oundle on 4 May 1964; and Oundle to Peterborough on 6 November 1972. Today the section from Yarwell Junction to Peterborough forms the Nene Valley Railway opening to passengers on 30 June 1986. The station at Peterborough is approximately on the same site as the original L&BR station.   *K. Fairey*

Stanier Class 5 No 44935 awaits departure from the rebuilt station at Coventry with the 6.1pm all stations local to Northampton on 29 April 1963. This view, in the shadow of Coventry's famous 'Three Spires', was shortlived – new office blocks were to obscure the view soon after it was taken. Although Coventry station and its associated installations received no serious damage in the wartime bombing of the city, by the end of the last war they had become inadequate for the passenger and parcels traffic of the district. The station and track layout received their last major improvements in the 1880s. Since then the population has more than quadrupled. The reconstruction at Coventry passenger station was begun in earnest on 10 August 1959, with the demolition of the luggage lifts and parcels bridge. The design of the station, in the hands of BR's Regional Architect, was considered to be an exciting architectural renaissance, continuing the great tradition of the Victorian railway architects translated into the language of the 20th century. The new station was in full use by May 1962.

Ray Reed

BR Standard Class 4 No 75011 heads the 5.10pm from Coventry to Nuneaton past Websters Sidings on 15 April 1963. Opened by the London & Birmingham Railway on 12 September 1850, the Nuneaton line has always been important for mineral traffic. Passenger services between Leamington & Nuneaton were withdrawn on 18 January 1965. Intermediate stations on the line have been demolished, but the Leamington to Coventry section reopened for passengers on 2 May 1977 and from Coventry to Nuneaton on 11 May 1987, the new station at Bedworth officially opening on 10 May 1988.   *Paul Riley*

Far Left: A wide variety of loads and rolling stock is captured here in this fast-disappearing scene taken at Stechford on 14 October 1961. Aston (21D) MPD-based Stanier Class 5 No 44865, blowing off furiously, toys with a few wagons – a fascinating, but, by then, an increasingly uneconomic operation.   *M. Mensing*

Left: Rugby (2A) MPD's Stanier Class 5 No 44909 arrives at Birmingham New Street on 15 June 1963. At this time the centre of Birmingham was in the throes of reconstruction. The new Rotunda building was taking shape as part of the city centre's infamous 'Bullring' development – a then new and ultimately less than successful project – which is currently being developed yet again. Prior to August 1959 the limited clearances in the tunnel between the station and Proof House Junction had prevented the use of LMS Pacifics into New Street. Coinciding with the city centre's redevelopment, this situation was rectified when a new concrete shell was constructed at a height of 90ft over the tunnel and after a series of controlled explosions had demolished the old brickwork, the structure was left, giving the necessary clearances for overhead electrification.

The inauguration of electric traction took place on 6 March 1967 and simultaneously heralded the opening of the reconstructed passenger station at New Street. The electric services had begun between Rugby, Coventry, Wolverhampton High Level and Stafford, and between Colwich and Stone.

Work on the main contract at New Street had begun in April 1964. The eight through and six bay platforms were replaced by 12 through platforms, and Queen's Drive, which had formerly divided the station, was replaced by one of the new island platforms. All passenger amenities, booking offices, refreshment rooms and staff accommodation were at concourse level.

W. Potter

Above: This grand old lady, LNWR 0-8-0 Class G2A No 48895, was a familiar sight to enthusiasts in the Wolverhampton area in the early 1960s where she is seen pottering about in the former Midland Railway yard at Wednesfield Road Goods Depot in November 1961. During the course of her lifetime No 48895 underwent no fewer than three rebuilds. Constructed as LNWR No 1585 in 1904, she was rebuilt as a Class E four cylinder compound in 1906 and was changed into a two cylinder simple engine with superheat in May 1921. In April 1944 she was again rebuilt with higher boiler pressure and increased braking power and was classified as Class G2A, and was not withdrawn until December 1964 after 60 years' service.   *D. Chaplin*

Right: The rebuilding of Bescot MPD in 1952 in the classic 'louvre' style made it indistinguishable from other sheds dealt with similarly by the LMS. The contract, issued in April 1951 to Edward Wood & Sons had been for 'renewal of the roof, pits and pavings.' This view, taken on 1 October 1961, shows some of the surviving 'Super D' 0-8-0s.   *T. B. Owen*

Left: 'Super D' 0-8-0 No 49361 is seen at the head of an SLS railtour on 22 June 1963 near Norton Canes, between Norton Junction and East Cannock Junction. The name 'Super D' arose from the fact that these engines (their correct classification being G1 and G2/G2A depending on boiler pressure) were a superheated version of the LNWR 'D' Class. In terms of height, the LNWR loading gauge was fairly generous and from 1928 many 0-8-0s had their cabs modified to the slightly more restricted ex-Midland Railway loading gauge. No 49361 has been fitted with a tender cab,

a modification made to some members of the class which were used for local trip freights between marshalling yards. These trips often involved much tender-first running which could be very uncomfortable for the crew in bad weather. Withdrawal of the class only commenced in 1947 with Class G2A No 9336 after a collision at Rugby. The last five survivors ended their days working from Bushbury and Bescot, some of the final examples having started life, nominally at least, over 60 years earlier as four-cylinder compounds.

R. Hobbs

Above: A rare view in colour of Aston (3D) MPD photographed on 4 May 1958. Twenty-five years earlier, in May 1933, Aston was one of 13 LMS depots authorised for modernisation. These modifications were generally thought to be an approximation of the layout at Camden where arrangements of 1) Watering 2) Coaling 3) Dropping Fire 4) Turning 5) Inspection, prior to disposal were introduced to permit a much quicker turnround of engines at sheds. The depot at Aston closed on 11 October 1965 and the site has been redeveloped as a commercial vehicle depot. *W. Potter*

Blackpool (24E) MPD's Ex-Works Stanier Class 5 No 44926 is depicted on the Rugeley to Walsall line south of Cannock on 17 June 1962. This up Birmingham parcels train was diverted over this route owing to pre-electrification work on the Stafford to Birmingham route. Opened in 1859, this line passed through the Cannock Chase coalfield and served the collieries in that area which were noted for their antiquated industrial locomotives from obscure builders. The railway today is still double track and until recently was busy with merry-go-round coal trains for which the remaining collieries in the area served the local power stations. Closed to passenger services on 18 January 1965, the remaining stations have since been demolished.

M. Mensing

BR Standard Class 5 No 73025 heads the 6.24pm Stafford to Wellington service near Donnington on 29 August 1964. Treated by the LNWR as their through route to Wales, this cross-country line was opened by the Shropshire Union Railway on 1 June 1849. The line was closed to passenger services just nine days after this picture was taken on 7 September, freight services between Stafford and Newport being withdrawn on 1 August 1966 – the Newport to Donnington section closing to freight on 1 July 1968. The Newport to Donnington section has been converted to a footpath, the line between Wellington and Donnington has recently been dismantled. Stations on the branch have been demolished; the site at Newport is a housing development incorporating the old station. *M. Mensing*

Above: A strong LNWR presence is visible in this view of Buxton (9D) MPD taken on 6 October 1962. Close to the town and yet surrounded by open fields (as the site is today) the depot at Buxton was thoroughly modernised with an earlier design of steel ash lifting plant and a concrete coal-bunker. Whilst LMS (and later BR) roofs were remade in the 'single pitch' style, and were followed by the 'louvre' pattern, in general terms an odd hybrid crept in. This was presumably a specific contractor's design as similar arrangements were followed by the LNER at Cambridge and at other locations. Buxton MPD was closed on 4 March 1968, together with the depots at Northwich (8E) and Trafford Park (9E). *N. Fields*

Right: Former North London Railway 0-6-0 Tank No 58856 heads an SLS special over the Cromford & High Peak line on 25 April 1953. Ex-LNER 'J94' Austerity 0-6-0s started to edge the NLR tanks out in April 1956. A diesel was tried and found to be very much wanting in 1959, the line eventually closing in April 1967. *J. M. Jarvis*

With less than a month before withdrawal, Bolton (9K) MPD's BR Standard Class 5 No 73026 is being prepared for railtour duty at Chester (6A) MPD on 4 March 1967. A total of 172 of this class were constructed between 1951 and June 1957. These locomotives were based on the LMS Class 5 design, but contained a number of detail alterations including the high running-plate, cab layout, regulator control, three bar crosshead, 6ft 2in coupled wheels and top feed. Enginemen's opinions of theses machines varied. Naturally, Ex-LMS men preferred the Stanier version, while SR crews found the Standards to be strong and reliable locomotives. Today, five members of the class survive – Nos 73050, 73082, 73096, 73129 and 73156.

Derek Huntriss

The strategic importance of the Shrewsbury & Crewe Railway, opened on 1 September 1858, dramatically increased with the opening of the Severn Tunnel in 1886. It enabled the LNWR and GWR to break the Midland's monopoly of West of England services via Birmingham and Bristol. The route retained its shape until 1970 when long-distance services were switched via Birmingham. Since then Shrewsbury and Crewe have been served by Manchester/Liverpool-Cardiff trains. Here, Stanier Pacific No 46239 *City of Chester* enters Whitchurch with 1V54, the 9.30am Manchester to Swansea, in August 1963. *D. Penney*

One of the last two Hughes/Fowler 'Crabs' to remain in operational service, No 42942, is depicted outside Birkenhead (8H) MPD on 4 March 1967. The 'Crab' was designed for both passenger and freight train operations. For the locomotive to get the necessary tractive effort from its 5ft 6in dia wheels, large cylinders were needed. In turn this brought loading gauge problems which required the cylinders to be steeply inclined in order to clear station platforms. Another feature popular with footplate staff was the roomy cab with double side windows, as in the later LYR style. From the mid-1930s, the 2-6-0s were eclipsed by the Stanier Class 5s, and were more commonly used on freight workings except at weekends when they were utilised for holiday passenger trains. However, some Scottish crews felt that the 'Crabs' were the best machines the LMS ever sent to Scotland, and that included the Class 5 4-6-0s. Withdrawal of the Hughes/Fowler 'Crabs' commenced in July 1961, all being taken from traffic by January 1967. However, three of this class have been preserved.

Derek Huntriss

Stanier Class 8F No 48465 passes the LNWR Type 4 box at Hooton South on 4 November 1967. This box, constructed in 1902, had 128 levers. The largest box on the LNWR was Euston No 2, with 288 levers in two frames with the men working back to back. In strange contrast to the large scale of the LNWR boxes, the name was inscribed on the front below the windows in small cast iron letters, sometimes not even mounted on a board.

Derek Huntriss

Left: Stanier Class 5 No 45305 stands at the head of an LCGB railtour at Liverpool Lime Street on 6 April 1968. Electric trains between Crewe and Liverpool were inaugurated on 18 June 1962, the event marking the completion of the second stage of the LMR main line 25kV electrification. This meant that all local passenger services between Crewe and Liverpool were provided by electric multiple units and all through trains which stopped at Crewe were headed from there by 3,300hp Type A locomotives on the electrified lines to Liverpool and Manchester. Power supply comes from two feeder stations, one at Speke, the other at Crewe. Similarly, there are two District Electric Depots, one at Crewe and the other at Allerton, where electric locomotives undergo short-term examination and light repairs and servicing. *Ray Reed*

Below: 'Jubilee' 4-6-0 No 45669 *Fisher* departs from Runcorn with an up express in August 1959. Runcorn was better known for its bridge over the River Mersey, a structure that was opened on the evening of Thursday May 21 1868. This towering structure was closed, one track at a time, prior to electrification in 1961 allowing deck plates to be renewed and the track to be relaid on ballast instead of longitudinal bolsters. *D. Penney*

Above: Stockport Edgeley (9B) MPD's Fowler 2-6-4T No 42379 passes Bradley Junction near Huddersfield with a Leeds to Stockport local on 27 August 1959. Although the old 'North Western' route over the Pennines to Leeds was often considered to be something of a backwater, it can be said that a keen breed of enginemen came to maturity in this part of the West Riding of Yorkshire. Locomotives had to be well maintained in order to perform well on the steep climbs through the Pennines where road, railway, river and canal hug the same valley. *G. W. Morrison*

Right: One of the last surviving 'Jubilee' 4-6-0s No 45593 *Kolhapur* vigorously attacks the climb from Huddersfield to Standedge with a Saturday Scarborough to Manchester train on 2 September 1967. Standedge, the vast Pennine barrier which straddles the cross country route between Manchester and Leeds, is pierced by four tunnels, three of which carry the metals of the former LNWR line. The fourth carrying the waters of the Huddersfield canal was officially opened on 4 April 1811. Work on the railway tunnel began on 1 November 1849 and in all 1,953 men, 1,200 horses,

40 barges and four locomotives were used in its construction and it took exactly three years to complete.The second tunnel was opened in February 1871, six months earlier than planned. The third tunnel was a product of further traffic expansion and was undertaken by the LNWR itself giving a double line north of the previous tunnels. This work was officially opened on 5 August 1894, exactly four years from the lifting of the first sod. Today the single line tunnels have been taken out of use, closing on 30 October 1966. *Derek Huntriss*

Far Left: BR Standard Class 5 No 73069 climbs the 1 in 30 to Chequerbent on the Kenyon Junction to Bolton line on 6 June 1968. One of the earliest railways to be opened, the Bolton & Leigh Railway, was engineered by George Stephenson and opened on 1 August 1828, preceding the Manchester & Liverpool Railway by nearly two years. Built to provide a link with Bolton and the Leeds & Liverpool canal, the railway was engineered on canal lines with cable-worked inclines similar to those used on the Cromford & High Peak Railway. Daubhill and Chequerbent inclines remained until February 1885 when deviations opened with new stations replacing the early Bolton & Leigh buildings on both. The line became part of the LNWR in 1846 and had passenger services in operation until they were withdrawn by BR on 29 March 1954. The section from Tyldesley remained open for goods traffic until 6 January 1969, the line between Howe Bridge and Bickershaw Junction remaining in use until 11 February 1975. Most of the route from all the way round from Monton Green to Kenyon Junction in addition to the section from Tyldesley to Howe Bridge was converted to a footpath by the Greater Manchester Council. *N. Fields*

Left: The footplate crew of Stanier Class 5 No 44894 look on in amazement as their loco is prepared for duty by enthusiasts as it waits to take a freight from Windermere to Carnforth on the penultimate day of steam traction, 1 August 1968. The ten mile line from Oxenholme to Windermere is still in situ, although much of the station site at Windermere has been converted into a supermarket. In LMS days the line was considered to be the end of a main line with through services to Euston and in BR days a portion of the 'Lakes Express' served the line. The first branch to open in the Lake District, the line was authorised as the Kendal & Windermere Railway in 1845 and was worked by the Lancaster & Carlisle Railway. The Windermere branch opened for goods to Kendal on 4 January 1847 and through to Windermere on 21 April 1847. The L&C was leased to the LNWR in December 1859 with full amalgamation by Act of 21 July 1879. *Derek Huntriss*

Above: Stanier Class 5 No 44800 passes non-stop through Llandudno Junction with a train comprising mostly Southern Region stock on 31 July 1965. The station is the changing point for the scenic 28-mile long branch to Blaenau Ffestiniog where BR shares a station with the Ffestiniog Railway enabling the passenger to complete a through journey from North Wales to the Cambrian coast by connecting with the narrow gauge. The LNWR terminated at Blaenau Ffestiniog North station, about ¾ mile from the GWR's Central station on the line from Bala Junction. A new standard gauge link was opened on 20 April 1964, parallel to the then derelict Ffestiniog Railway.

P. W. Gray

Right: Against the backdrop of Conway Castle, BR Standard Class 5 No 73145 heads an up working, also on 31 July 1965. The North Wales estuary crossing at Conway offers a splendid spectacle of engineering with the medieval castle harmonising well with Telford's road suspension and Stephenson's tubular railway bridges.

P. W. Gray

Left: Class 5 4-6-0 No 45184 crosses the River Severn as it leaves Shrewsbury station with an up passenger working on 17 July 1965. With the completion of the Newport, Abergavenny & Hereford Railway soon after 1853, a short route between South Wales and the North became available and came under the joint control of the LNWR and GWR in 1862. The LNWR by that time had its own access to Shrewsbury from Crewe which opened in 1858. These arrangements were not affected upon Nationalisation, the lines remaining in the London Midland and Western Regions respectively, but from 9 September 1963, the whole Shrewsbury district came under the control of the LMR. The original joint station was built at the north end of the bridge over the Severn. Gradually enlarged in the last century, its platforms extended over the river.   *T. B. Owen*

Above: Fairburn 2-6-4T No 42267 prepares to leave Shrewsbury station with the 3.10pm all stations service to Wellington and Stafford on 17 August 1963. With the introduction of electric hauled services on the West Coast main line many major locomotives classes were relegated to other duties, the Shrewsbury to Stafford locals often being in the hands of 'Jubilee' and 'Britannia' class locomotives.   *J. Duncan Gomersall*

73

Above: BR Standard Class 4 2-6-4T No 80097 takes water at Builth Road High Level as it works the 3pm Shrewsbury to Swansea (Victoria) on 21 August 1962. Over this long and picturesque route there were still five passenger trains daily at this time; the most important being the 'York Mail' conveying through coaches from Swansea (Victoria) to York via Stockport, Stalybridge and Leeds.   *P. W. Gray*

Right: Ex-LNWR 'Coal Tank' No 58888 is depicted outside Abergavenny (86K) MPD on 6 September 1953. 'Coal Tanks' always formed a large proportion of the allocation at Abergavenny, 28 being on the books in 1912, 37 in August 1919 and as late as December 1947 as many as nine were still to be found. Before Nationalisation in 1948, the Abergavenny & Merthyr line had been serviced by the old 4-road

engine shed at Abergavenny, coded (31) by the LNWR and later (4D) by the LMS, becoming (86K) under British Railways. The last of the class to remain in service at Abergavenny, No 58926, had its final active duty on 5 January 1958 when it worked a special last train from Abergavenny to Merthyr for the Stephenson Locomotive Society, although it was not officially withdrawn until October 1958.   *T. B. Owen*

This view of 0-6-0PT No 9675 outside Dowlais Central No2 Junction box is looking north towards the point where the LNWR 'Heads of the Valleys' line came in from the right to join the Brecon & Merthyr. In the distance beyond the bridge can be seen the signal-box controlling the LNWR junction. Today a large part of the Abergavenny to Merthyr line is now the A465 'Heads of the Valleys' road built over the trackbed from Beaufort to Dowlais Top. In addition to the road there is a footpath from Llanfoist to Gilwern with platforms and station houses surviving at Govilon, Gilwern and Clydach.

A. A. Jarvis

BR Standard Class 5 No 73095 prepares to leave Swansea (Victoria) with the 9.45am train for Shrewsbury on 25 April 1963. In the 1900s the Central Wales line was worked by Webb 5ft 6in 2-4-2 Ts which were reported to be prone to an unpleasant rolling motion when running at speed down the banks. These engines were assisted with heavy trains over those sections northbound from Llandovery and Builth by the faithful old 'DXs.' From about 1911 these were superseded by Cooke's large 4-6-2 side tanks which were thought to have been built primarily for Central Wales services .   *A. A. Jarvis*

Below: Preserved LNWR 2-4-0 'Jumbo' *Hardwicke* is seen outside Steamtown MPD at Carnforth in October 1974. *Hardwicke's* place in history was its epic performance on the night of 22 August 1895, when the 141 miles from Crewe to Carlisle were run in 126 minutes, the fastest start to stop average recorded during the Races to Aberdeen. The load was, of course, light, but no lighter in relation to the size of the engine when compared to other well-publicised runs with more

modern steam motive power. It is estimated that in climbing from Carnforth to Shap summit, *Hardwicke* sustained an estimated 635 i.h.p. The second best known member of this class was No 955 *Charles Dickens* which between its construction in 1882 and withdrawal in 1912 completed over 2,300,000 miles in traffic.

Derek Huntriss

Right: Webb 'Coal Tank' No 1054 is seen climbing the 1 in 58 out of Keighley in July 1986. Built at Crewe works in 1888 it became LMS No 7799 at the Grouping being withdrawn in 1939 and later reinstated. Following restoration at Crewe Works in 1961 it has been kept at various locations including the Hednesford depot of the RPS, Penrhyn Castle museum and Dinting Railway Centre, where it was fully restored.

D. Huntriss

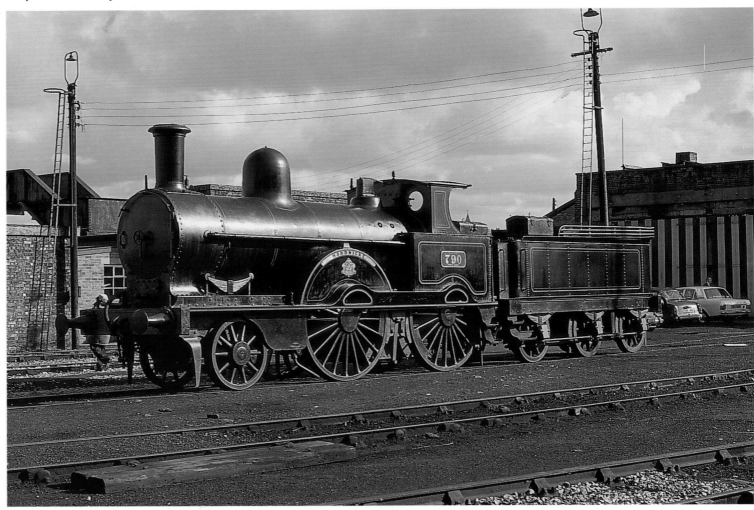

Railway Classics from IAN ALLAN *Publishing*

The Heyday of Leeds Holbeck & its Locomotives
By Gavin Morrison ISBN: 0711022259 7.5in x 9.5in Paper over board **£10.99**

The Heyday of Steam Around Manchester
By Tom Heavyside ISBN: 0711023298 7.5in x 9.5in Paper over board **£10.99**

The Heyday of the DMU
By Alan Butcher ISBN: 0711023190 7.5in x 9.5in Paper over board **£10.99**

The Heyday of Old Oak Common & its Locomotives
By Chris Leigh ISBN: 0711021430 7.5in x 9.5in Paper over board **£10.99**

The Heyday of Nine Elms & its Locomotives
By Colin Boocock ISBN: 0711020671 7.5in x 9.5in Paper over board **£10.99**

Southern EMUs in Colour
By John C. Morgan ISBN: 0711023182 7.5in x 9.5in Paper over board **£10.99**

On London & South Western Lines
By Alan C. Butcher ISBN: 071102331X 7.5in x 9.5in Paper over board **£10.99**

Bulleid Locomotives in Colour
By Rex Kennedy ISBN: 0711021864 7.5in x 9.5in Paper over board **£10.99**

Industrial Steam
ISBN: 0711022305 7.5in x 9.5in Paper over board **£10.99**

On Great Central Lines
By Robert Robotham ISBN: 0711022445 7.5in x 9.5in Paper over board **£10.99**

On Cambrian Lines
By Derek Huntriss ISBN: 0711021856 7.5in x 9.5in Paper over board **£10.99**

On Great Northern Lines
By Derek Huntriss ISBN: 0711022860 7.5in x 9.5in Paper over board **£10.99**